Mandala Coloring Book V.1

Stress Reliever

Andrea T. Cross

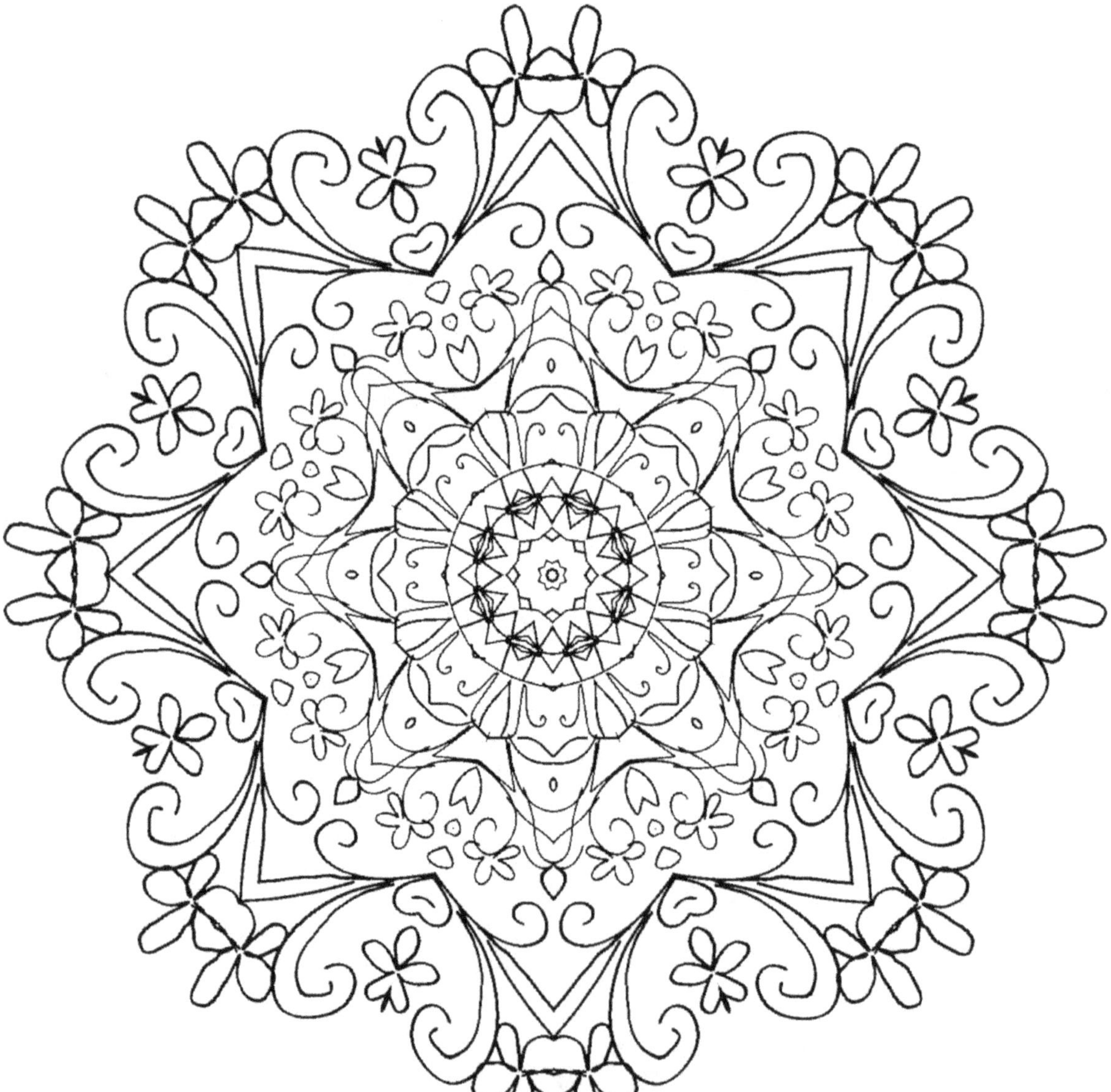

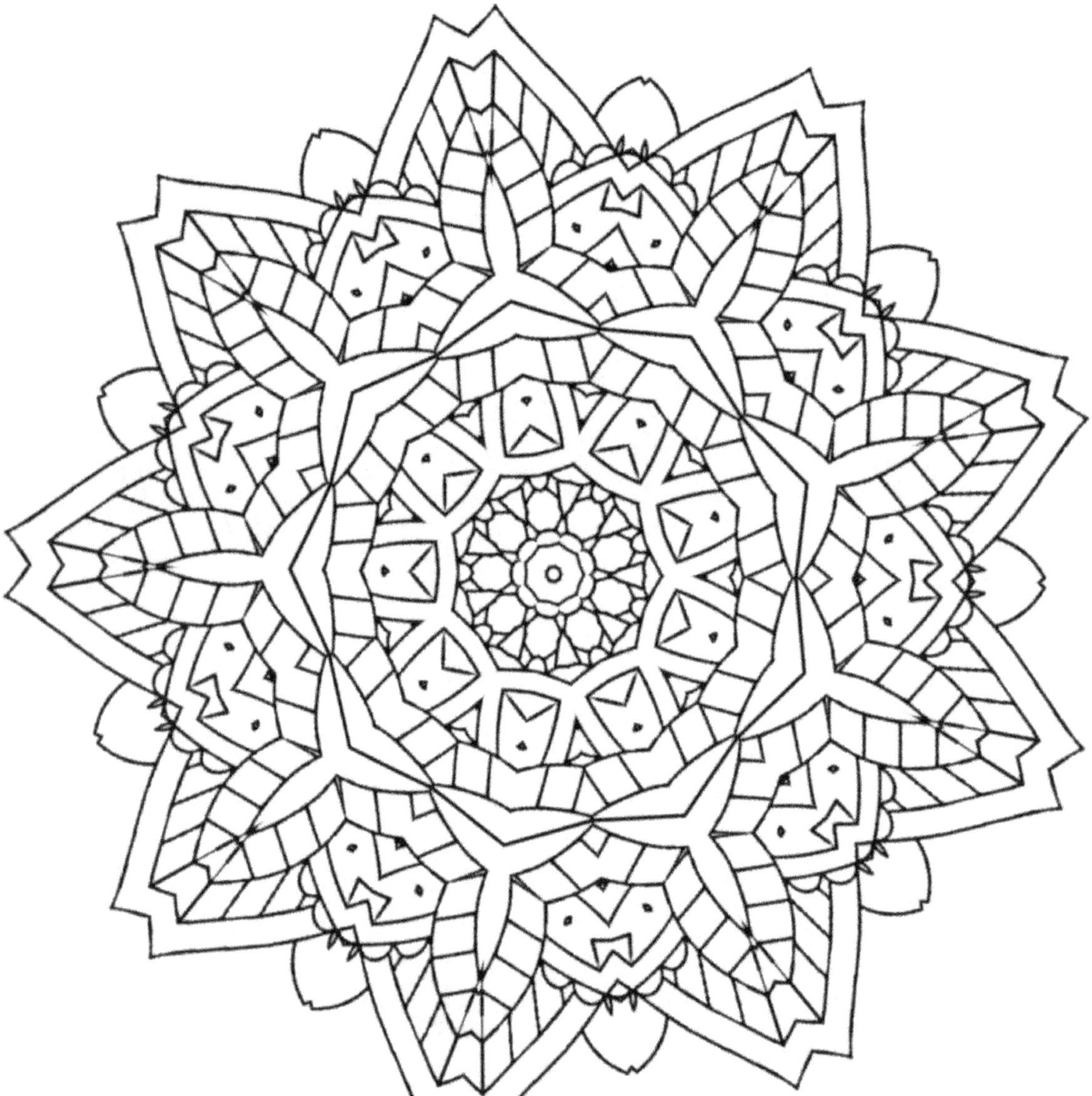

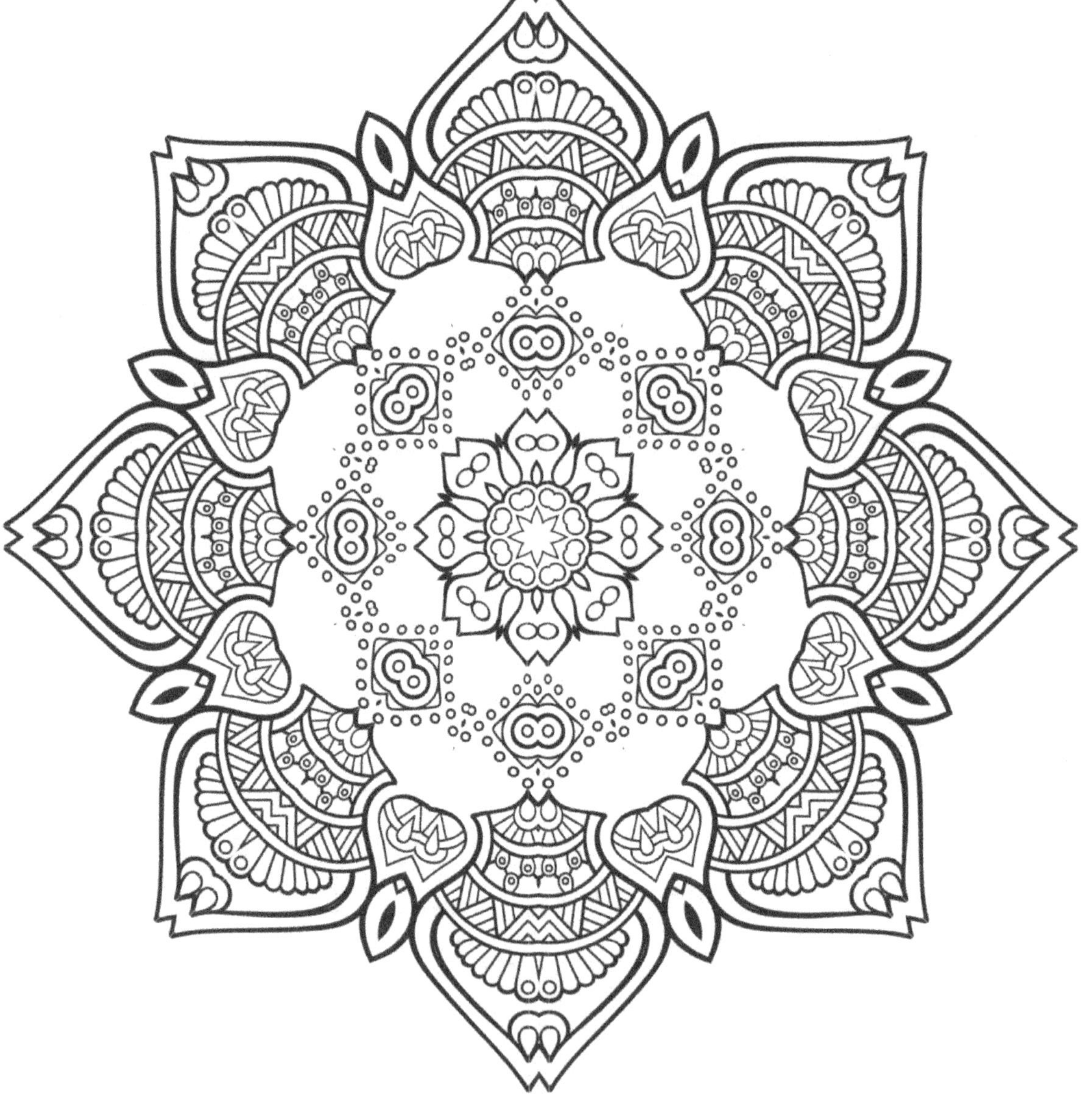

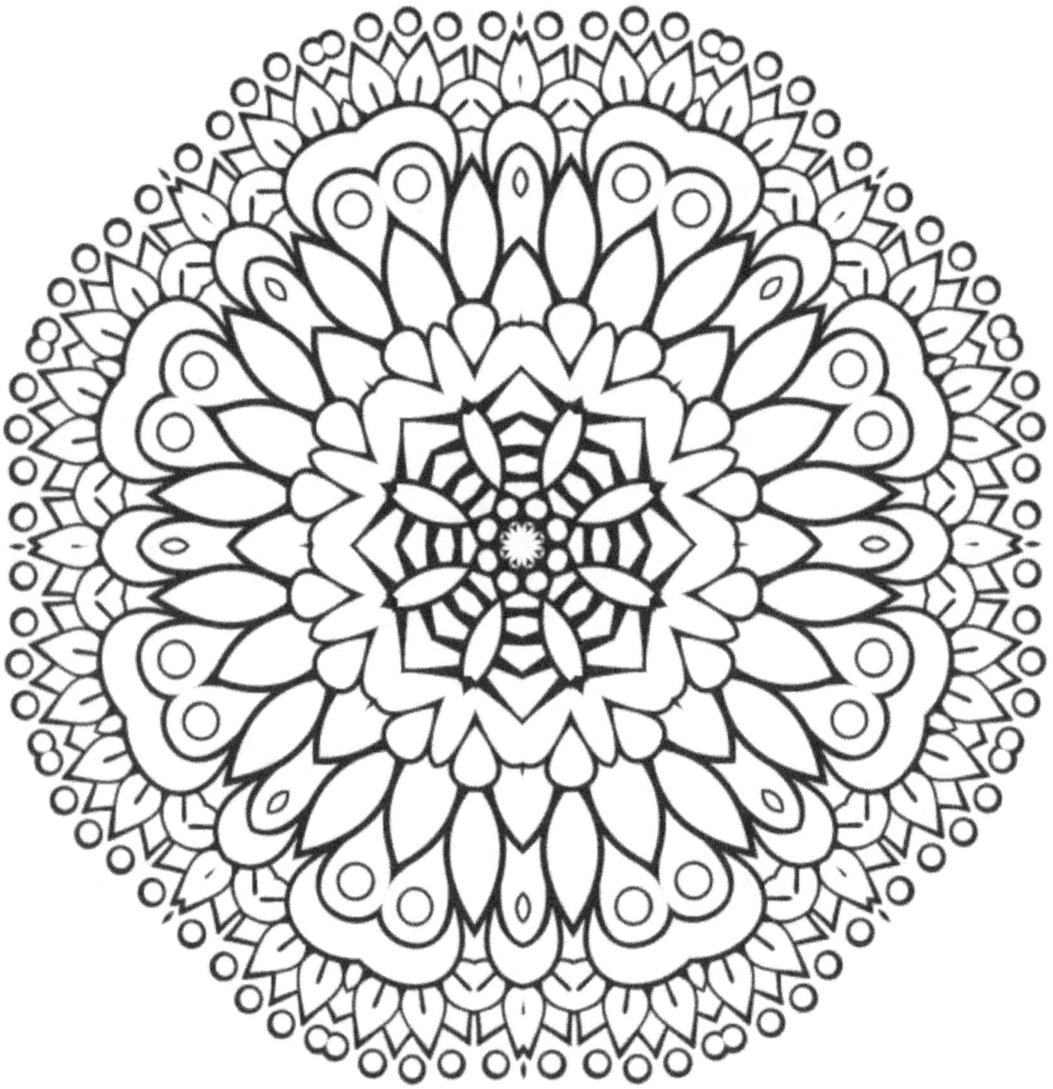

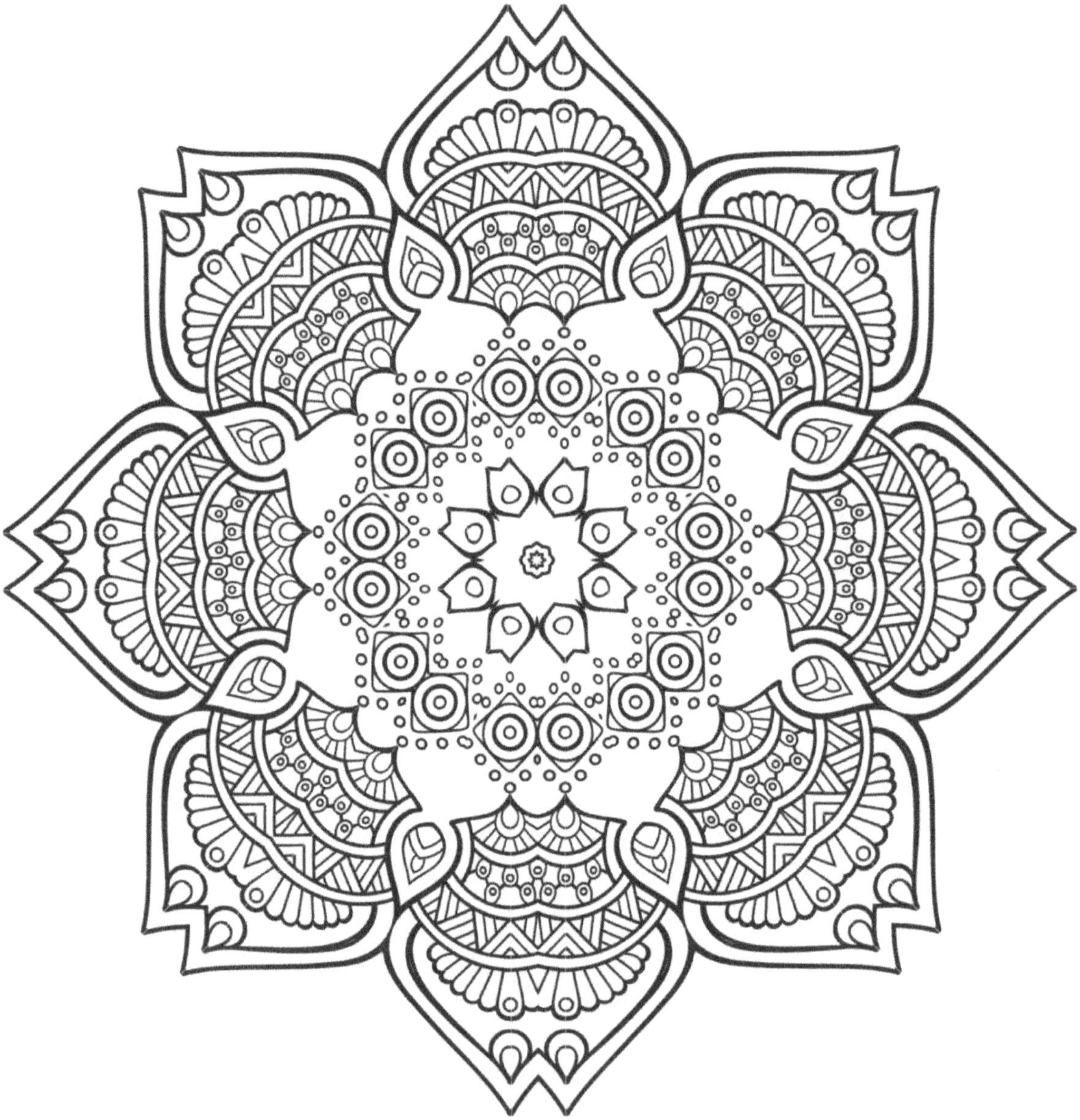

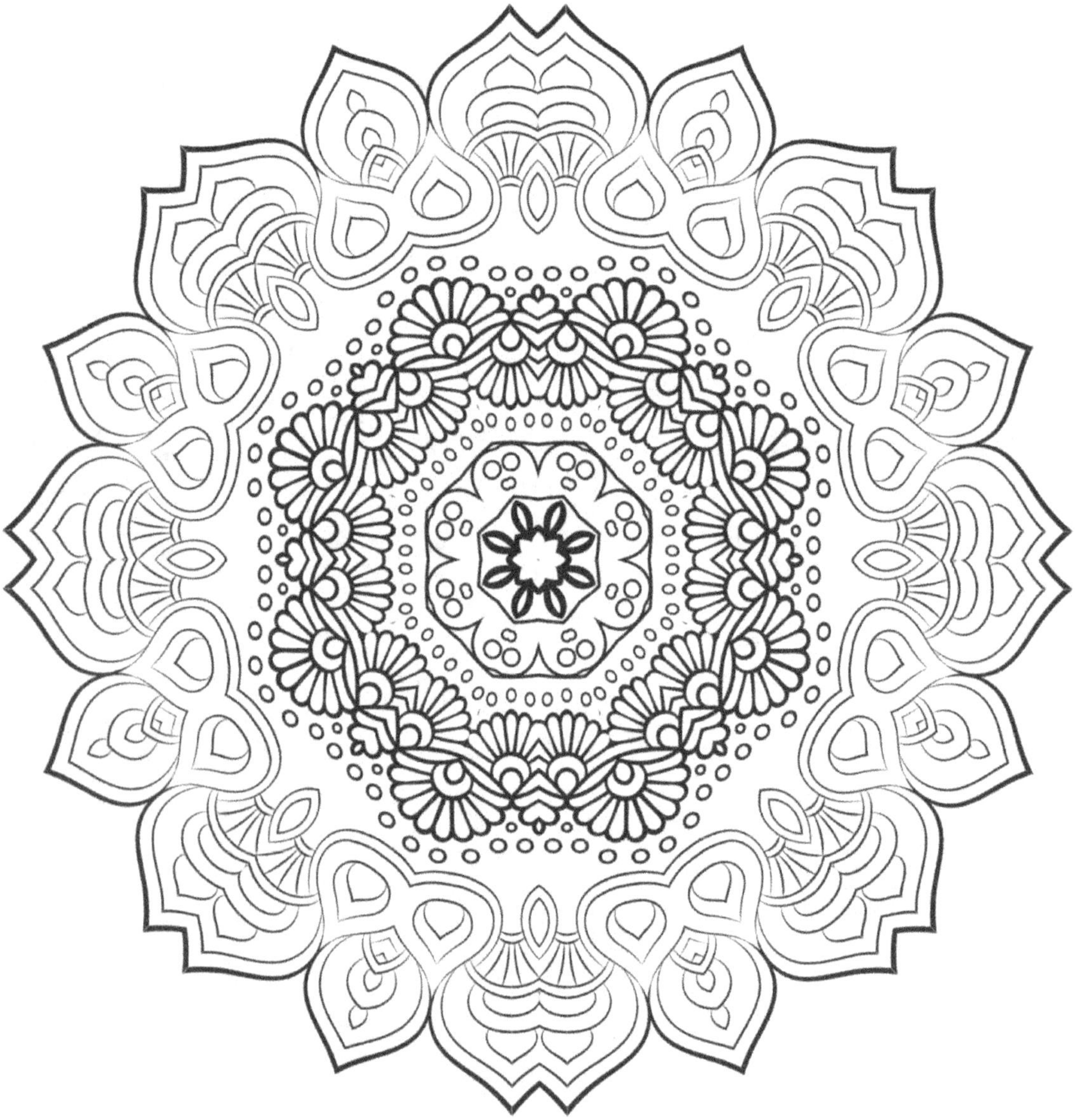

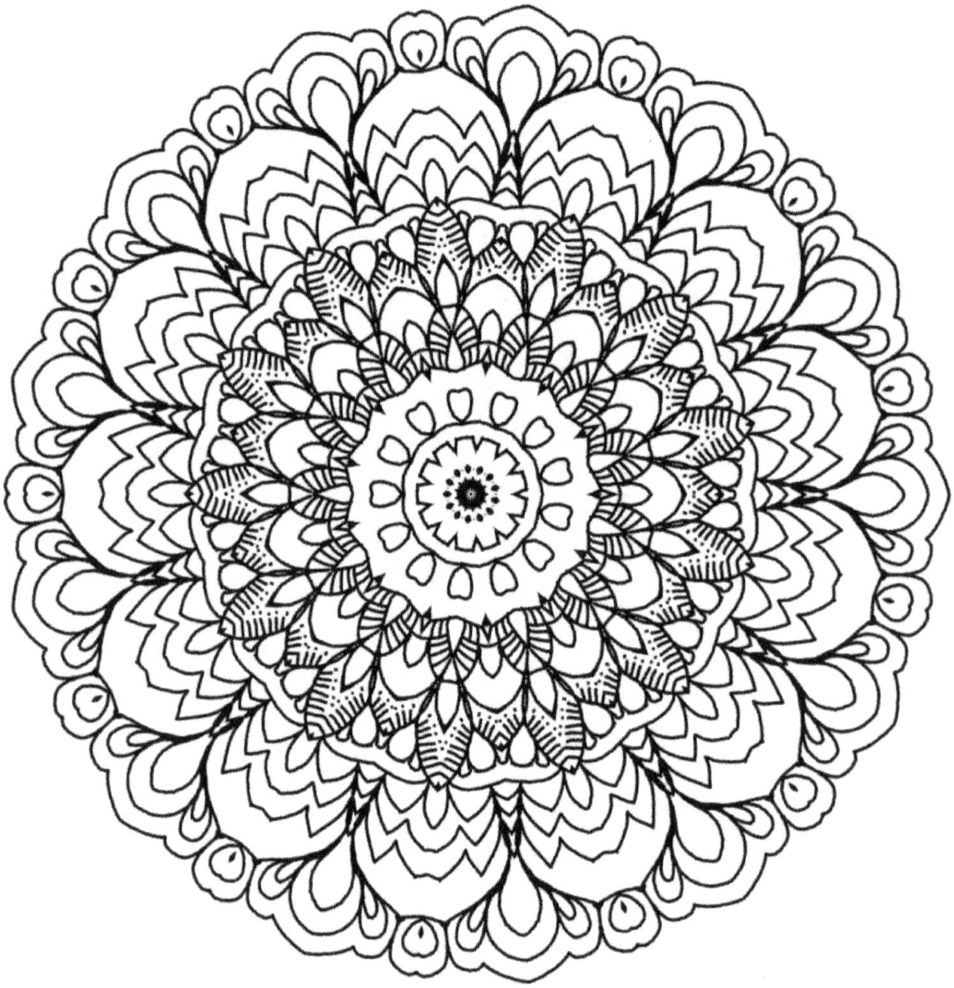

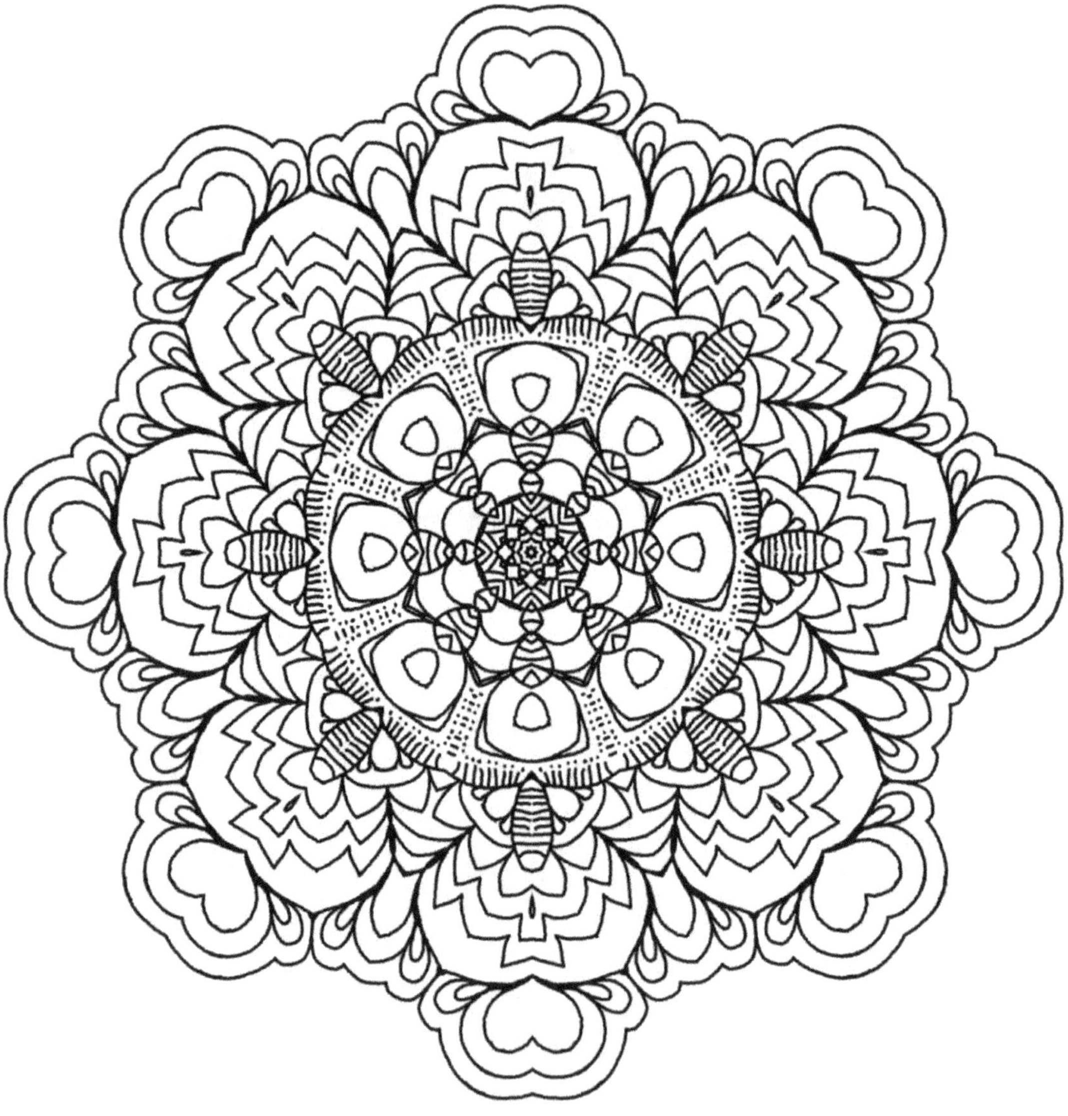

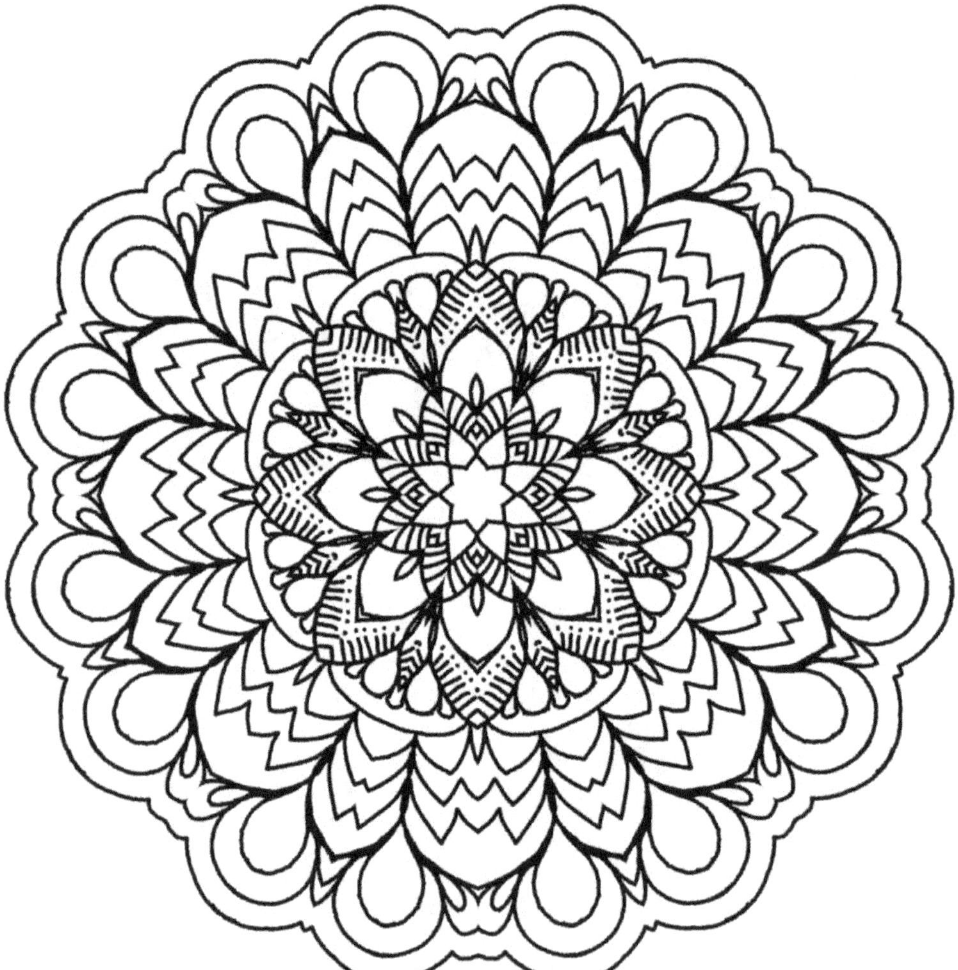

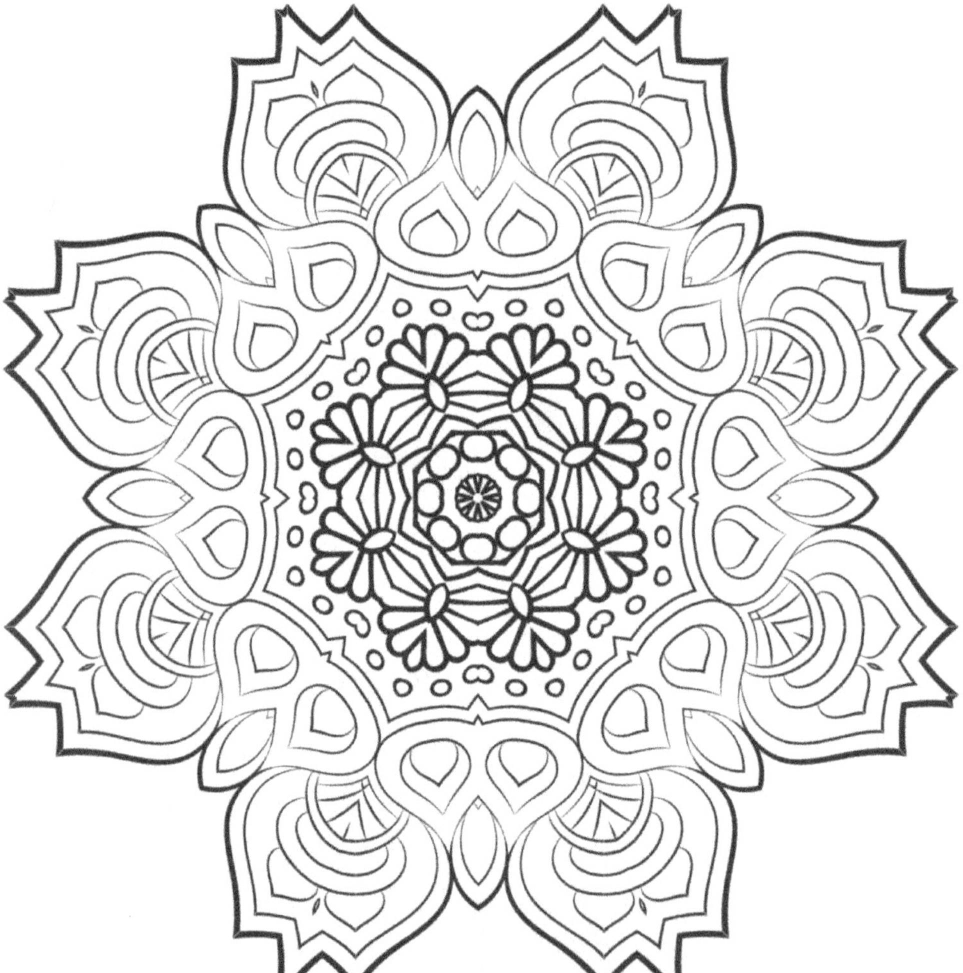

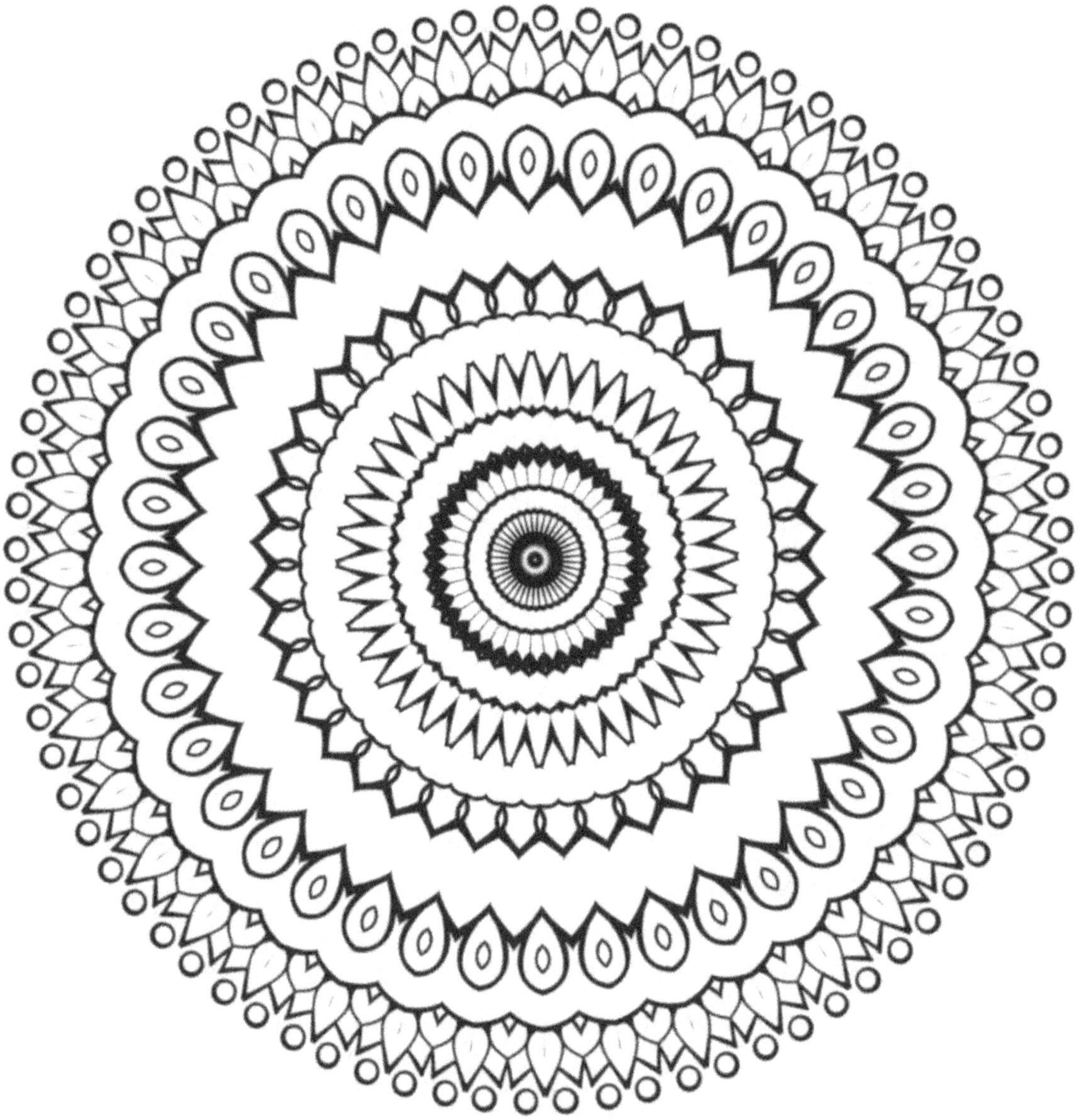

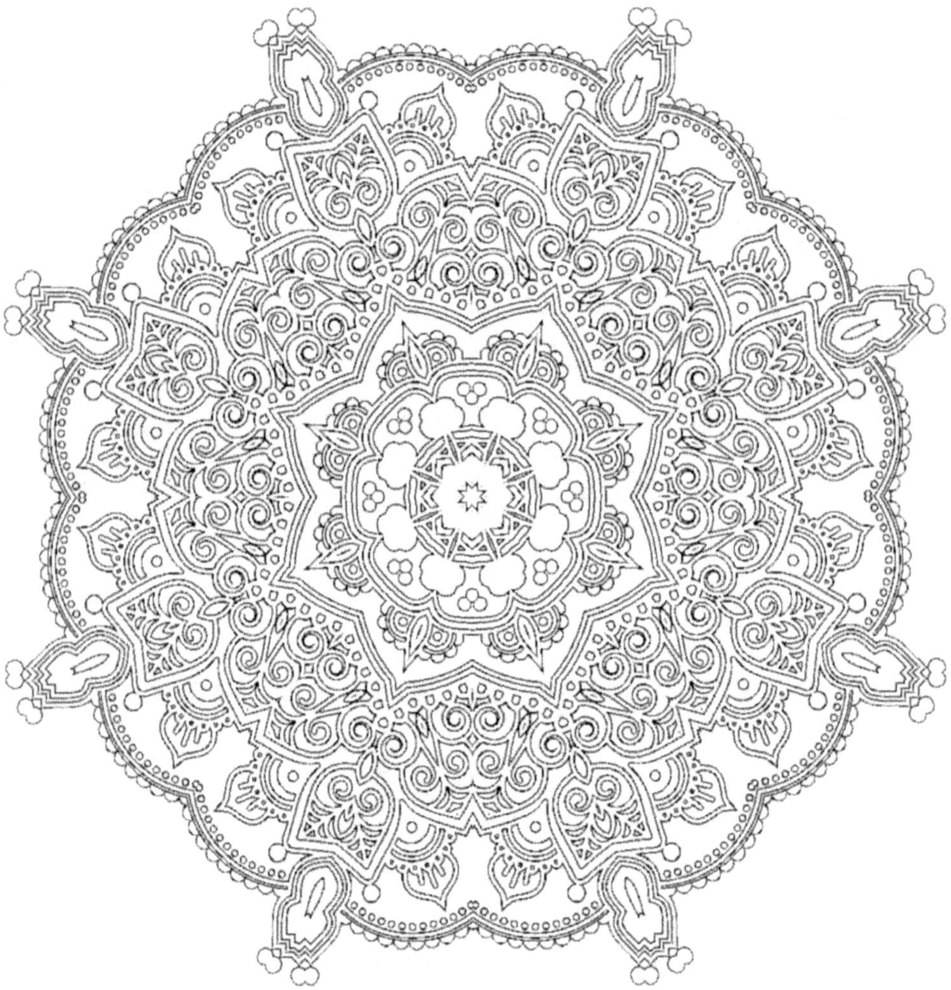

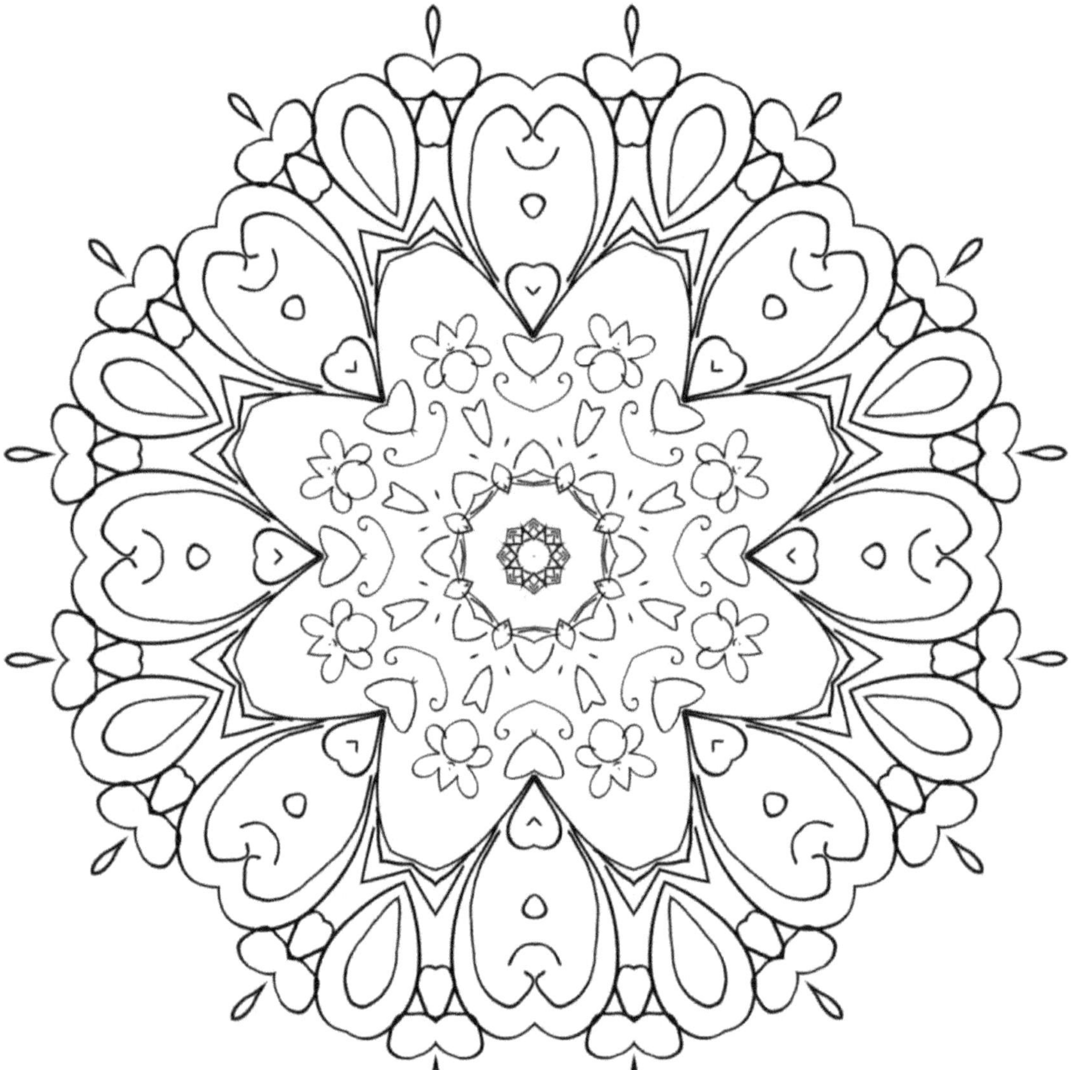

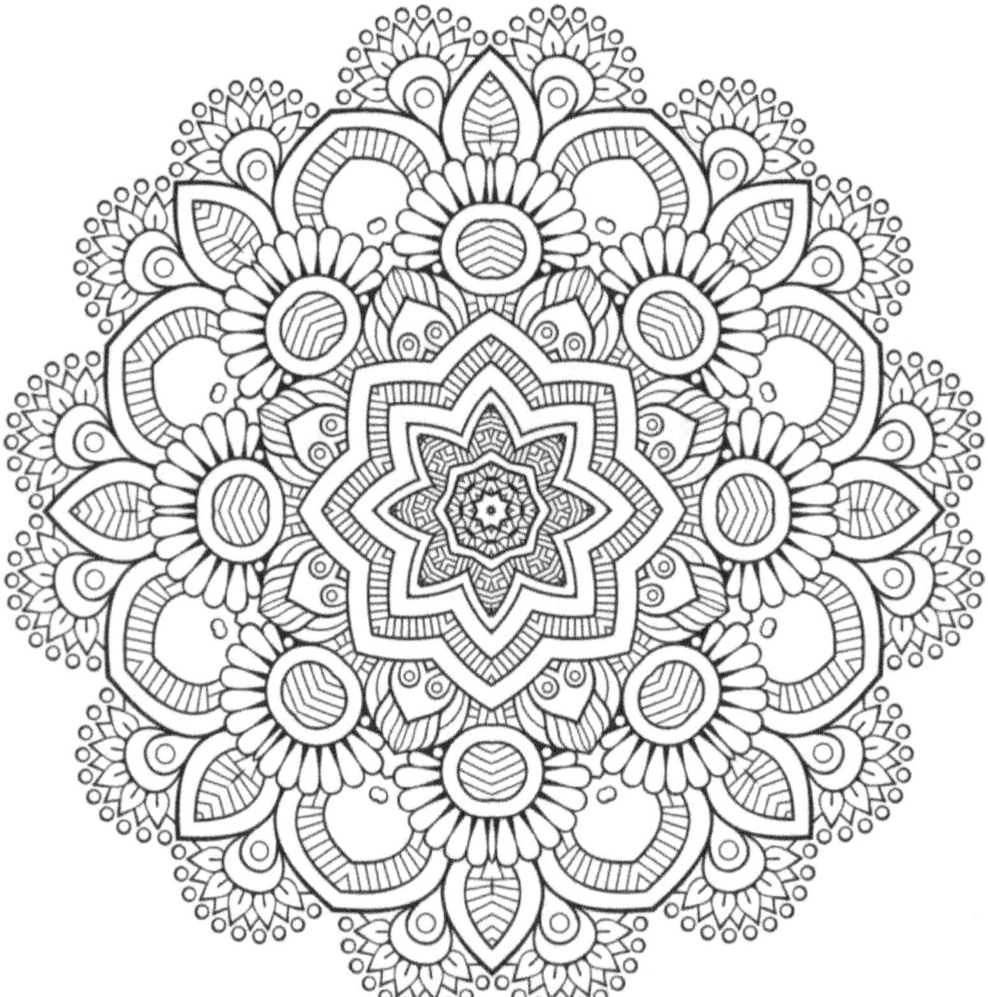

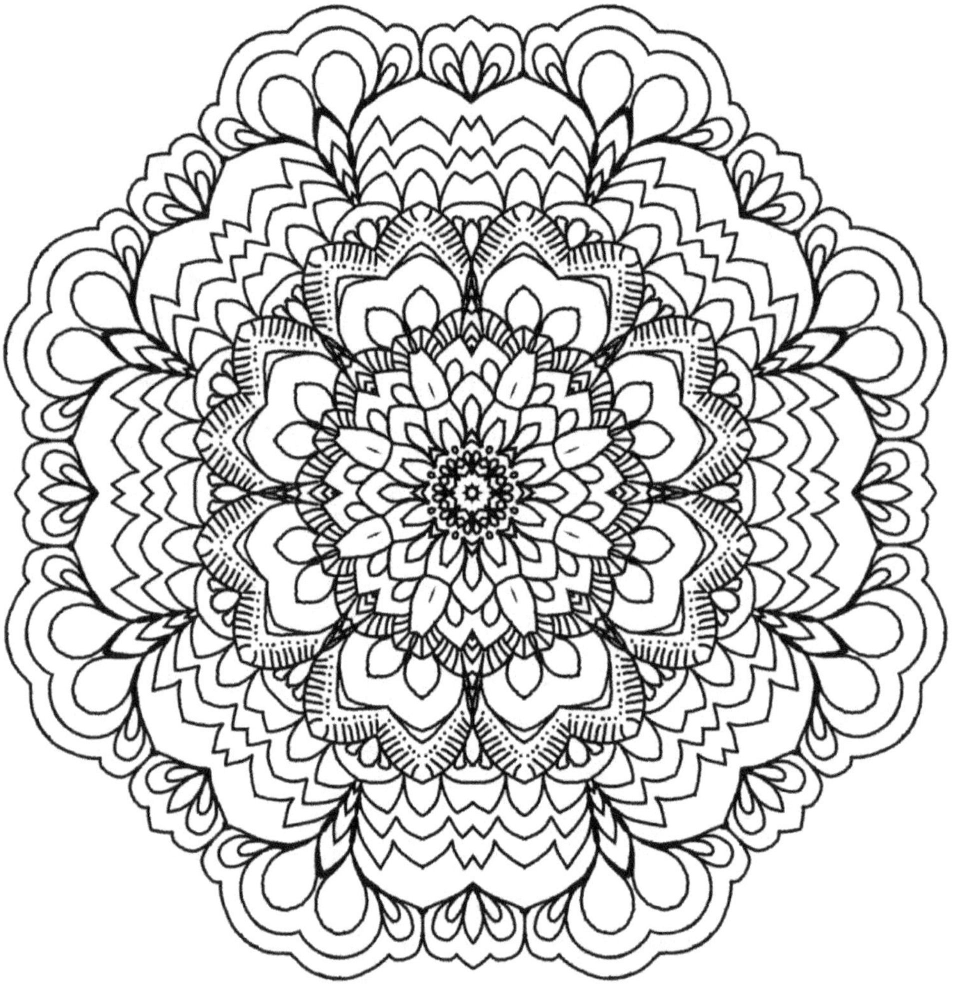

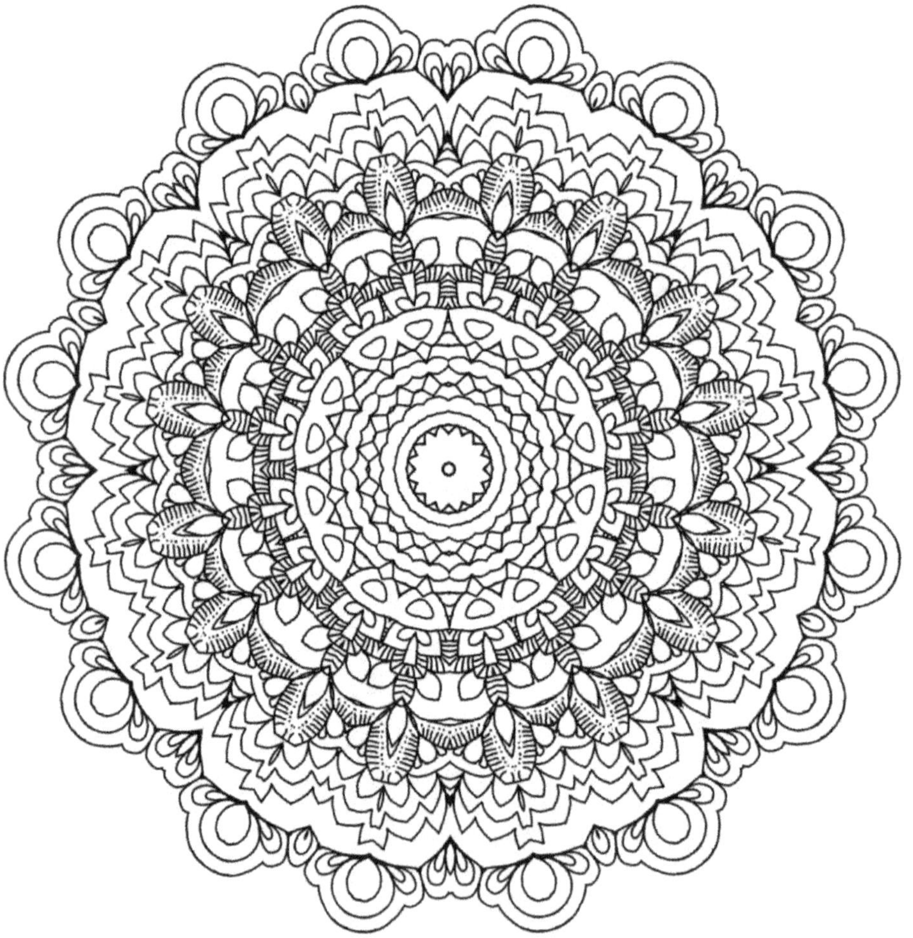

www.ingramcontent.com/pod-product-compliance
Lightning Source LLC
Chambersburg PA
CBHW081024170526
45158CB00010B/3147
* 9 7 8 1 0 8 9 5 0 7 2 3 9 *